On Happiness

Pierre Teilhard de Chardin

On Happiness

Translated by René Hague

Collins
St James's Place, London
1973

Sur le Bonheur
was first published in 1966 by
Editions du Seuil

© Editions du Seuil, 1966

© in the English translation
William Collins Sons & Co. Ltd.,
London, 1973

ISBN 0 00 215818 3

Made and printed in Great Britain by
William Collins Sons & Co. Ltd., Glasgow

Contents

Reflections on Happiness

In the world of mechanized matter, all bodies obey the laws of a universal gravitation; similarly, in the world of vitalized matter, all organized beings, even the very lowest, steer themselves and progress towards that quarter in which the greatest measure of well-being is to be found.

One might well imagine, then, that a speaker could hardly choose an easier subject than happiness. He is a living being addressing other living beings, and he might well be pardoned for believing that his audience contains none but such as are already in agreement with him and are familiar with his ideas.

In practice, however, the task I have set myself today turns out to be much nicer and more complex.

Like all other animate beings, man, it is true, has an essential craving for happiness. In man, however, this fundamental demand assumes a new and complicated form: for he is not simply a living being with greater sensibility and greater vibratory power than other living beings. By virtue of his 'hominization' he has become a reflective and critical living being; and his gift of reflection brings with it two other formidable properties, the power to perceive what may be possible, and the power to foresee the future. The emergence of this dual power is sufficient to disturb and confuse the hitherto serene and consistent ascent of life. Perception of the possible, and awareness of the future – when these two combine, they not only open up for us an inexhaustible store of hopes and fears, but they also allow those hopes and fears to range far afield in every direction. Where the animal seems to find no difficulties to obstruct its infallible progress towards what will bring it satisfaction, man, on the other hand, cannot take a single step in any direction without meeting a problem for which, ever since he became man, he has constantly and unsuccessfully been trying to find a final and universal solution.

'*De vita beata*', in the ancient phrase – on the happy life: what, in fact, is happiness?

For centuries this has been the subject of endless books, investigations, individual and collective experiments, one after another; and, sad to relate, there has been complete failure to reach unanimity. For many of us, in the end, the only practical conclusion to be drawn from the whole discussion is that it is useless to continue the search. Either the problem is insoluble – there is no true happiness in this world – or there can be only an infinite number of particular solutions – the problem itself defies solution. Being happy is a matter of personal taste. You, for your part, like wine and good living.

I prefer cars, poetry, or helping others. 'Liking is as unaccountable as luck.' You must often, I am sure, have heard that sort of remark, and it may well be that you are a little inclined to agree.

What I want to do this evening is to confront fairly and squarely this relativist (and basically pessimist) scepticism shared by so many of our contemporaries, by showing you that, even for man, the general direction in which happiness lies is by no means so ill-defined as it is taken to be: provided always that we confine our enquiry to the search for those joys which are essential and, in so doing, take as our basis what we are taught by science and biology.

I cannot, unfortunately, give you happiness: but I do hope that I may be able at least to help you to find it.

What I have to say falls into two parts. In the first, which will be primarily theoretical, we shall try together to define the best route leading to human happiness.

In the second part, which will serve as a conclusion, we shall consider how we must adapt our individual lives to these general axes which run towards happiness.

I. THE THEORETICAL AXES OF HAPPINESS

A. The Root of the Problem: Three Different Attitudes to Life

If we are to understand more clearly how the problem of happiness presents itself to us, and why we find ourselves at a loss when we meet it, it is essential to start by taking a comprehensive view of the whole position. By this I mean that we must distinguish three fundamental initial attitudes to life adopted by men as a matter *of fact*.

Here an analogy may well be a useful guide.

Let us imagine a party of tourists who have set out to climb a difficult peak, and let us take a look at them some hours after they have started. By this time we may suppose the party to be divided into three sorts of elements.

Some are regretting having left the inn. The fatigue and risks involved seem out of all proportion to the value of a successful climb. They decide to turn back.

Others are not sorry that they set out. The sun is shining, and there is a beautiful view. But what is the point of climbing any higher? Surely it is better to enjoy the mountain from here, in the open meadow or deep in the wood. And so they stretch out on the grass, or explore the neighbourhood until it is time for a picnic meal.

And lastly there are the others, the

real mountaineers, who keep their eyes fixed on the peaks they have sworn to climb.

The tired – the hedonists – the enthusiasts.

Three types of men: and, deep within our own selves, we hold the germ of all three. And, what is more, it is into these three types that the mankind in which we live and move has always been divided.

1. First, the Tired (or the Pessimists)

For this first category of men, existence is a mistake or a failure. We do not fit in – and so the best thing we can do is, as gracefully as possible, to retire from the game. If this attitude is carried to its extreme, and expressed in terms of a learned doctrinal system, it leads in the end to the wisdom of the Hindus, according to which the universe is an illusion and a prison – or to a pessimism such as Schopenhauer's. But, in a milder and commoner form, the same attitude emerges and can be recognized in any number of practical decisions that are only too familiar to you. 'What is the good of trying to find the answer? . . . Why not leave the savages to their savagery and the ignorant to their ignorance? What is the point of science? What is the point of the machine? Is it not better to lie down than to stand up? better to be dead than asleep in bed?' And all this amounts to saying, at least by implication, that it is better

16

to be less than to be more – and that best of all would be not to be at all.

2. Secondly, the Hedonists (or Pleasure-seekers)

For men of this second type, to be is certainly better than not to be. But we must be careful to note that in this case 'to be' has a special meaning. For the followers of this school, to be, or to live, does not mean to act, but simply to take your fill of this present moment. To enjoy each moment and each thing, husbanding it jealously so that nothing of it be allowed to be lost – and above all with no thought of shifting one's ground – that is what they mean by wisdom. When we have had enough, then we can lie back on the grass, or stretch our legs, or look at the view from another spot. And meanwhile, what is more, we shall not rule out the possibility of turning back downhill. We refuse, however, to risk anything for the sake of or on the chance of the future – unless, in an over-refinement of sensibility, danger incurred for its own sake goes to our heads, whether it be in order to enjoy the thrill of taking a chance or to feel the shuddering grip of fear.

This is our own version, in an over-simplified form, of the old pagan hedonism found in the school of Epicurus. In literary circles such has recently been the tendency, at any rate, of a Paul Morand or a Montherlant – or (and here it is far more subtle) of a Gide (the Gide of *Fruits of the Earth*), whose ideal of life is to drink without ever quenching (rather, indeed, in such a way as to increase) one's thirst – and this with no idea of restoring one's vigour, but simply from a desire to drain, ever more avidly, each new source.

3. Finally, the Enthusiasts

By these I mean those for whom living is an ascent and a discovery. To men in this third category, not only is it better to be than not to be, but they are convinced that it is always possible – and the possibility has a unique value – to attain a fuller measure of being. For these conquerors, enamoured of the adventurous, being is inexhaustible – not in Gide's way, like a precious stone with innumerable facets which one can never tire of turning round and round – but like a focus of warmth and light to which one can always draw closer. We may laugh at such men and say that they are ingenuous, or we may find them tiresome; but at the same time it is they who have made us what we are, and it is from them that tomorrow's earth is going to emerge.

Pessimism and return to the past; enjoyment of the present moment; drive towards the future. There, as I was saying, we have three fundamental attitudes to life. Inevitably, therefore, we find ourselves back at the very heart of our subject: a confrontation between three contrasting forms of happiness.

1. First, the Happiness of Tranquillity

No worry, no risk, no effort. Let us cut down our contacts, let us restrict our needs, let us dim our lights, toughen our protective skin, withdraw into our shell. – The happy man is the man who attains a minimum of thought, feeling and desire.

2. Secondly, the Happiness of Pleasure

Static pleasure or, better still, pleasure that is constantly renewed. The goal of life is not to act and create, but to make use of opportunities. And this again means less effort, or no more effort than is needed to reach out for a clean glass or a fresh drink. Lie back and relax as much as possible, like a leaf drinking in the rays of the sun – shift your position constantly so that you may feel more fully: that is the recipe for happiness. – The happy man is the man who can savour to the highest degree the moment he holds in his hands.

3. Finally, the Happiness of Growth

From this third point of view, happiness has no existence nor value in itself, as an object which we can pursue and attain as such. It is no more than the sign, the effect, the reward (we might say) of appropriately directed action: a by-product, as Aldous Huxley says somewhere, of effort. Modern hedonism is wrong, accordingly, in suggesting that some sort of renewal of ourselves, no matter what form it takes, is all that is needed for happiness. Something more is required, for no change brings happiness unless the way in which it is effected involves an *ascent*. – The happy man is therefore the man who, without any direct search for happiness, inevitably finds joy as an added bonus in the act of forging ahead and attaining the fullness and finality of his own self.

Happiness of tranquillity, happiness of pleasure, and happiness of development: we have only to look around us to see that at the level of man it is between these three lines of progress that life hesitates and its current is divided.

Is it true, as we are so often told, that our choice is determined only by the dictates of individual taste and temperament?

Or is the contrary true? that somewhere we can find a reason, indisputable because objective, for deciding that one of these three roads is absolutely the best, and is therefore the only road which can lead us to real happiness?

B. The Answer Given by the Facts

1. *General Solution: Fuller Consciousness as the Goal*

For my part, I am absolutely convinced that such a criterion, indisputable and objective, does exist – and that it is not mysterious and hidden away but lies open for all to see. I hold, too, that in order to see it all we have to do is to look around and examine nature in the light of the most recent achievements of physics and biology – in the light, that is, of our new ideas about the great phenomenon of evolution.

The time has come, as you must know, when nobody any longer retains any serious doubts about this:

25

the universe is not 'ontologically' fixed – in the very depths of its entire mass it has from the beginning of time been moving in two great opposing currents. One of these carries matter towards states of extreme disintegration; the other leads to the building up of organic units, the higher types of which are of astronomical complexity and form what we call the 'living world'.

That being so, let us consider the second of these two currents, the current of life, to which we belong. For a century or more, scientists, while admitting the reality of a biological evolution, have been debating whether the movement in which we are caught up is no more than a sort of vortex, revolving in a closed circle; or whether it corresponds to a clearly defined drift, which carries the animate portion of the world towards some specific higher state. There is today almost unanimous agreement that it is the second of these hypotheses which would appear undoubtedly to correspond to reality. Life does not develop complexity without laws, simply by chance. Whether we consider it as a whole or in detail, by examining organic beings, it progresses methodically and irreversibly towards ever higher states of consciousness. Thus the final, and quite recent, appearance of man on the earth is only the logical and consistent result of a process whose first stages were already initiated at the very origins of our planet.

Historically, life (which means in fact the universe itself, considered in its most active portion) is a rise of consciousness. How this proposition directly affects our interior attitudes and ways of behaviour must, I suggest, be immediately apparent.

We talk endlessly, as I was saying a moment ago, about what is the best attitude to adopt when we are confronted by our own lives. Yet, when we talk in this way, are we not like a passenger in the Paris to Marseilles express who is still wondering whether he ought to be travelling north or south? We go on debating the point: but to what purpose, since the decision has already been taken without reference to ourselves, and here we are on board the train? For more than four hundred million years, on this earth of ours (or it would be more correct to say, since the beginning of time, in the universe), the vast mass of beings of which we form a part has been tenaciously and tirelessly climbing towards a fuller measure of freedom, of sensibility, of inner vision. And are we still wondering whither we should be bound?

The truth is that the shadow of the false problems vanishes in the light of the great cosmic laws. Unless we are to be guilty of a physical contradiction (unless, that is, we deny everything that we are and everything that has made us what we are) we are all obliged, each of us on his own account, to accept the primordial choice which is built into the world of which we are the reflective elements. If we withdraw in order to diminish our being, and if we stand still to enjoy what we have, in each case we find that the attempt to run counter to the universal stream is illogical and impossible.

The road to the left, then, and the road to the right are both closed: the only way out is straight ahead.

Scientifically and objectively, only one answer can be made to the demands of life: the advance of progress.

In consequence, and again scientifically and objectively, the only true happiness is the happiness we have described as the happiness of growth and movement.

Do we want to be happy, as the world is happy, and with the world? Then we must let the tired and the pessimists lag behind. We must let the hedonists take their homely ease, lounging on the grassy slope, while we ourselves boldly join the group of those who are ready to dare the climb to the topmost peak. Press on!

Even so, to have chosen the climb is not enough. We have still to make sure of the right path. To get up on our feet ready for the start is well enough. But, if we are to have a successful and enjoyable climb, which is the best route?

Here again, if we are to be sure of our ground, we must see how nature proceeds – we must learn from the sciences of life.

2. Detailed Solution: the Three Phases of Personalization

As I said earlier, life in the world continually rises towards greater consciousness, proportionate to greater complexity – as though the increasing complexity of organisms had the effect of deepening the centre of their being.

Let us consider, then, how this advance towards the highest unity actually works out in detail; and, for the sake of clarity and simplicity, let us confine ourselves to the case of man – man, who is physically the highest of all living beings and the one best known to us.

When we examine the process of our inner unification, that is to say of our personalization, we can distinguish three allied and successive stages, or steps, or movements. If man is to be fully himself and fully living, he must, (1) be centred upon himself; (2) be 'de-centred' upon 'the other'; (3) be super-centred upon a being greater than himself.

We must define and explain in turn these three forward movements, with which (since happiness, we have decided, is an effect of growth) three forms of attaining happiness must correspond.

1. First, *centration*. Not only physically, but intellectually and morally too, man is man only if he cultivates himself – and that does not mean simply up to the age of twenty . . .

If we are to be fully ourselves we must therefore work all our lives at our organic development: by which I mean that we must constantly introduce more order and more unity into our ideas, our feelings and our behaviour. In this lies the whole programme of action, and the whole value and meaning (all the hard work, too!) of our interior life, with its inevitable drive towards things that are ever-increasingly spiritual and elevated. During this first phase each one of us has to take up again and repeat, working on his own account, the general labour of life. Being is in the first place making and finding one's own self.

2. Secondly, *decentration*. An elemen-

tary temptation or illusion lies in wait for the reflective centre which each one of us nurses deep inside him. It is present from the very birth of that centre; and it consists in fancying that in order to grow greater each of us should withdraw into the isolation of his own self, and egoistically pursue in himself alone the work, peculiar to him, of his own fulfilment: that we must cut ourselves off from others, or translate everything into terms of ourselves. However, there is not just one single man on the earth. That there are, on the contrary, and necessarily must be, myriads and myriads at the same time is only too obvious. And yet, when we look at that fact in the general context of physics, it takes on a cardinal importance – for it means, quite simply, this: that, however individualized by nature thinking beings may be, each man still represents no more than an atom, or (if you prefer the phrase) a very large molecule; in common with all the other similar molecules, he forms a definite corpuscular system from which he cannot escape. Physically and biologically man, like everything else that exists in nature, is essentially plural. He is correctly described as a 'mass-phenomenon'. This means that, broadly speaking, we cannot reach our own ultimate without emerging from ourselves by uniting ourselves with others, in such a way as to develop through this union an added measure of

consciousness – a process which con-
forms to the great law of complexity.
Hence the insistence, the deep surge,
of love, which, in all its forms, drives
us to associate our individual centre
with other chosen and specially
favoured centres: love, whose essential function and charm are that it
completes us.

3. Finally, *super-centration*. Although
this is less obvious, it is absolutely
necessary to understand it.

If we are to be fully ourselves, as I
was saying, we find that we are
obliged to enlarge the base on which
our being rests; in other words, we
have to add to ourselves something
of 'the Other'. Once a small number
of centres of affection have been

initiated (some special circumstances determining their choice), this expansive movement knows no check. Imperceptibly, and by degrees, it draws us into circles of ever-increasing radius. This is particularly noticeable in the world of today. From the very beginning, no doubt, man has been conscious of belonging to one single great mankind. It is only, however, for our modern generations that this indistinct social sense is beginning to take on its full and real meaning. Throughout the last ten millennia (which is the period which has brought the sudden speeding-up of civilization) men have surrendered themselves, with but little reflection, to the multiple forces (more profound than any war) which were gradually bringing them into closer contact with one another; but now our eyes are opening, and we are beginning to see two things. The first is that the closed surface of the earth is a constricting and inelastic mould, within which, under the pressure of an ever-increasing population and the tightening of economic links, we human beings are already forming but one single body. And the second thing is that through the gradual building-up within that body of a uniform and universal system of industry and science our thoughts are tending more and more to function like the cells of one and the same brain. This must inevitably mean that as the transformation follows its natural line of progress we can foresee the time when men will understand what it is, animated by one single heart, to be united together in wanting, hoping for, and loving the same things at the same time.

The mankind of tomorrow is emerging from the mists of the future, and we can actually see it taking shape: a 'super-mankind', much more conscious, much more powerful, and much more unanimous than our own. And at the same time (a point to which I shall return) we can detect an underlying but deeply rooted feeling that if we are to reach the ultimate of our own selves, we must do more than link our own being with a handful of other beings selected from the thousands that surround us: we must form one whole with all simultaneously.

We can draw but one conclusion from this twofold phenomenon which operates both outside ourselves and inside ourselves: that what life ultimately calls upon us to do in order that we may be, is to incorporate ourselves into, and to subordinate ourselves to, an organic totality of which, cosmically speaking, we are no more than conscious particles. Awaiting us is a centre of a higher order – and already we can distinguish it – not simply beside us, but *beyond* and *above* us.

We must, then, do more than develop our own selves – more than give ourselves to another who is our equal – we must surrender and attach

41

our lives to one who is greater than ourselves.

In other words: first, be. Secondly, love. Finally, worship.

Such are the natural phases of our personalization.

These, you must understand, are three linked steps in life's upward progress; and they are in consequence three superimposed stages of happiness – if, as we have agreed, happiness is indissolubly associated with the deliberate act of climbing.

The happiness of growing greater – of loving – of worshipping.

Taking as our starting-point the laws of life, this, to put it in a nutshell, is the triple beatitude which is theoretically foreseeable.

Now what is the verdict of experience on this point. Let us for a moment go directly to the facts, and use them to check the accuracy of our deductions.

First, there is the happiness of that deep-seated growth in one's own self – growth in capabilities, in sensibility, in self-possession. Then, too, there is the happiness of union with one another, effected between bodies and souls that are made to complete one another and come together as one.

I have little need to emphasize the purity and intensity of these two first forms of joy. Everybody is in basic agreement on that point.

But what shall we say about the happiness of sinking and losing self

in the future, in one greater than
ourselves?... Is not this pure theoriz-
ing or dreaming? To find joy in what
is out of scale with us, in what we can
as yet neither touch nor see. Apart
from a few visionaries, is there any-
one in the positivist and materialist
world we are forced to live in who
can concern himself with such an
idea?

Who, indeed?

And yet, consider for a moment
what is happening around us.

Some months ago, at a similar
meeting, I was telling you about the
two Curies – the husband and wife
who found happiness in embarking
on a venture, the discovery of
radium, in which they realized that
to lose their life was to gain it. Just

think, then: how many other men (in a more modest way, maybe, and in different forms and circumstances), yesterday and today, have been possessed, or are still possessed, even to the point of death, by the demon of research? Try to count them.

In the Arctic and Antarctic: Nansen, Andrée, Shackleton, Charcot, and any number of others.

The men of the great peaks: the climbers of Everest.

The laboratory workers who ran such risks: killed by rays or by the substances they handled – victims of a self-injected disease.

Add to these the legion of aviators who conquered the air.

And those, too, who shared man's

conquest of man: all who risked, or indeed gave, their lives for an idea.[1]

Make a rough count; and when you have done so, take the writings and letters left by these men (such of them as left any), from the most noteworthy of them (the everyday names) to the most humble (those whose names are not even known) – the airmail pilots who twenty-five years ago were pioneering the air-route across America for human thoughts and loves, and paid for it, one after another, with their lives. What do you find when you read

[1] 'You know that my life is an oblation, joyfully and conscientiously offered, with no selfish hope of reward, to the Power which is higher than life.' (Rathenau)

what they confided to paper? You find joy, a joy that is both higher and deeper – a joy full of power: the explosive joy of a life that has at last found a *boundless* area in which to expand.

Joy, I repeat, in that which knows no bounds.

What generally saps and poisons our happiness is that we feel that we shall so soon exhaust and reach the end of whatever it is that attracts us: we know the pain of separation, of loss by attrition – the agony of seeing time fly past, the terror of knowing how fragile are the good things we hold, the disappointment of coming so soon to the end of what we are and of what we love.

But when a man has found, in

an ideal or a cause, the secret of collaboration and self-identification (whether it be close or distant) with the universe as it advances, then all those dark shadows disappear. The joy of worshipping so spreads over the joy of being and the joy of loving as to allow them to expand and grow firmer (Curie, for example, and Termier were admirable friends, fathers and husbands): it does not lessen or destroy the earlier joys, and it holds and brings with it, in its fullness, a wonderful peace. Its source of nourishment is inexhaustible, because it gradually becomes one with the very consummation of the world in which we move; by the same token, moreover, it is safe from every threat of death and decay.

Finally, it is, in one way or another, constantly within our reach, since the best way we have of reaching it is simply, each one of us in his own place, to do what we are able to do as well as we can.

The joy of the element which has become conscious of the whole which it serves and in which it finds fulfilment – the joy which the reflective atom draws from awareness of its function and completion within the universe which contains it – this, both logically and factually, is the highest and most progressive form of happiness I can put before you and hope that you may attain.

2. THE FUNDAMENTAL RULES OF HAPPINESS

So much for pure theory. We may now consider in what ways it can be applied to our individual lives.

We have just made it clear that true happiness is a happiness of growth – and, as such, it awaits us in a quarter characterized by:

1. unification of self within our own selves;

2. union of our own being with other beings who are our equals;

3. subordination of our own life to a life which is greater than ours.

What consequences do these definitions entail for our day-to-day conduct? And what practical action should we take in order to be happy?

I can, of course, satisfy your curiosity and assist your good will by only the most general indications; for it is here that, quite rightly, we come up against any number of problems of taste, accident and temperament. Life becomes established and progresses in nature and structure only by reason of the very great variety of its elements. Each one of us sees the world and makes his approach to it from a particular angle, backed by a reserve of vital energy, with its own peculiarities, which cannot be shared by others. (We may note, incidentally, that it is this complementary diversity which underlies the biological value of 'personality'.) Each one of us, therefore, is the only person who can ultimately discover for himself the attitude, the approach (which nobody else can imitate), which will make him cohere to the utmost possible degree with the surrounding universe as it continues its progress; that cohesion being, in fact, a state of peace which brings happiness.

Bearing these reservations in mind, we can, following our earlier lines of thought, draw up the following three rules of happiness.

1. If we are to be happy, we must first react against our tendency to follow the line of least resistance, which causes us either to remain as we are, or to look primarily to activities external to ourselves for what will provide new impetus to our

lives. We must, it is true, sink our
roots deep into the rich, tangible,
material realities which surround
us; but in the end it is by working to
achieve our own inner perfection
– intellectual, artistic, moral – that
we shall find happiness. The most
important thing in life, Nansen used
to say, is to find oneself. Through
and beyond matter, spirit is hard at
work, building. – *Centration*.

2. If we are to be happy we must,
secondly, react against the selfishness which causes us either to close
in on ourselves, or to force our
domination upon others. There is a
way of loving – a bad and sterile way
– by which we try to possess rather
than to give ourselves. Here again,

in the case of the couple or the group, we meet that same law of maximum effort which governed the progress of our interior development. The only love which brings true happiness is that which is expressed in a spiritual progress effected in common. – *Decentration*.

3. And if we are to be happy – completely happy – we must, thirdly, in one way or another, directly or through some medium which gradually reaches out further afield (a line of research, a venture, an idea, perhaps, or a cause), transfer the ultimate interest of our lives to the advancement and success of the world we live in. If we are to reach the zone where the great permanent

sources of joy are to be found, we must be like the Curies, like Termier and Nansen, like the first aviators and all the pioneers I spoke of earlier: we must re-polarize our lives upon one greater than ourselves. Do not be afraid that this means that if we are to be happy we must perform some remarkable feat or do something quite out of the ordinary; we have only to do what any one of us is capable of: become conscious of our living solidarity with one great Thing, and then do the smallest thing in a great way. We must add one stitch, no matter how small it be, to the magnificent tapestry of life; we must discern the Immense which is building up and whose magnetic pull is exerted at the very heart of our own humblest activities and at their term; we must discern it and cling to it – when all is said and done, that is the great secret of happiness. As one of the most acute, and most materialist, thinkers of modern England, Bertrand Russell, has put it: it is in a deep and instinctive union with the whole current of life that the greatest of all joys is to be found. – *Super-centration.*

There you have the real core of what I have to say to you; but, having reached that point, there is one more thing which I owe it to you and to myself to say, if I am to be absolutely truthful.

I was recently reading a curious

book,[1] in which the English novelist and thinker H. G. Wells writes about the original views recorded earlier by an American biologist and businessman, William Burrough Steele, which bear precisely on the point we are now considering, human happiness. Steele tries, with much good sense and cogency, to show (just as I have been doing) that since happiness cannot be dissociated from some notion of immortality, man cannot hope to be fully happy unless he sinks his own interests and hopes in those of the world, and more particularly in those of mankind. He adds, however, that, put in those terms, the solution is still incomplete;

[1] H. G. Wells, *The Anatomy of Frustration.*

for if we are to be able to make a complete gift of self we must be able to love. And how can one love a collective, impersonal reality – a reality that in some respects must seem monstrous – such as the world, or even mankind?

The objection which Steele found when he looked deeper, and to which he gave no answer, is terribly and cruelly to the point. My treatment of the subject would, therefore, be both incomplete and disingenuous if I did not point out to you that the undeniable movement which, as we can see, is leading the mass of mankind to place itself at the service of progress is not 'self-sufficient': if this terrestrial drive which I am asking you to share is to be sustained, it must be harmonized and synthesized with the Christian drive.

We can look around and note how the mysticism of research and the social mysticisms are advancing, with admirable faith, towards the conquest of the future. Yet no clearly defined summit, and, what is more serious, no *lovable* object is there for them to worship. That is the basic reason why the enthusiasm and the devotion they arouse are hard, arid, cold, and sad: to an observer they can only be a cause for anxiety, and to those who aspire to them they can bring only an incomplete happiness.

At the same time, parallel with these human mysticisms, and until now only marginal to them, there is Christian mysticism; and for the last

two thousand years this has constantly been developing more pro-
foundly (though few realize this) its
view of a personal God: a God who
not only creates but animates and
gives totality to a universe which he
gathers to himself by means of all
those forces which we group together under the name of evolution.
Under the persistent pressure of
Christian thought, the infinitely dis-
tressing vastness of the world is
gradually converging upwards, to
the point where it is transfigured into
a focus of loving energy.

Surely, then, we cannot fail to see
that these two powerful currents
between which the force of man's
religious energies is divided – the
current of human progress, and the

current of all-embracing charity –
need but one thing, to run together,
and complete one another?

Suppose, first, that the youthful
surge of human aspirations, fan-
tastically reinforced by our new con-
cepts of time and space, of matter
and life, should make its way into the
life-stream of Christianity, enriching
and invigorating it; and suppose at
the same time, too, that the wholly
modern figure of a universal Christ,
such as is even now being developed
by Christian consciousness, should
stand, should burst into sight, should
spread its radiance, at the peak of our
dreams of progress, and so give them
precision, humanize and personalize
them. Would not this be an answer,
or rather *the* complete answer, to the

difficulties before which our action hesitates?

Unless it receives a new blood transfusion from matter, Christian spirituality may well lose its vigour and become lost in the clouds. And, even more certainly, unless man's sense of progress receives an infusion from some principle of universal love, it may well turn away with horror from the terrifying cosmic machine in which it finds itself involved.

If we join the head to the body – the base to the peak – then, suddenly, there comes a surge of plenitude.

To tell you the truth, I see the complete solution to the problem of happiness in the direction of a Christian humanism: or, if you prefer the phrase, in the direction of a super-human Christianity within which every man will one day understand that, at all times and in all circumstances, it is possible for him not only to serve (for serving is not enough) but to cherish in all things (the most forbidding and tedious, no less than the loveliest and most attractive) a universe which, in its evolution, is charged with love.

Lecture given by Père Teilhard de Chardin in Peking, 28 December 1943.

Three Wedding Addresses

*At the Wedding of Odette Bacot and Jean
Teilhard d'Eyry*

Mademoiselle, my dear Jean,

When I look at you both here,
united for all time, my old pro-
fessional habits reassert themselves,
and I cannot help glancing back at
the two roads – your two roads –
which for so long seemed to be inde-
pendent of one another; have just
suddenly converged, and here and
now, in a moment, are about to run
as one. And you will not be surprised
that, presented with a meeting so un-

expected and yet prepared for so long, I am filled with wonder and joy, as though I were witnessing another of life's triumphs.

Your road, Jean, began far from here, under the heavy clouds of the tropics, in the flat paddy-fields enclosed by the blue silhouette of Cape Saint-Jacques. It called for nothing less than this vigorous mixture of cold Auvergne and the Far East worthily to continue in you a fearless, far-ranging mother, and that legendary 'Uncle Georges' too. When I was only a child, I used occasionally to gaze with admiration at his face, beside the already white-haired grandmother, in that rather dark, and half-Chinese, drawing-room in the Rue Savaron.

By tradition, and by birth, you are of Asia; and that is why, from time to time, you have gone back to Asia to breathe in its quality.

But what are these journeyings of the heart and mind? Only you could draw up that itinerary, the stages and detours through which your being had to travel before the emergence in the end of the man you are today. At home, as a young cadet, everywhere, what influences were at work, what meetings came about, what attractions were felt, what choices made! . . . How slender the fibres in the web from which our lives are suspended!

Finally, having found your way through the shifting labyrinth of external and internal forces, you have

succeeded in finding your soul. In
this inner domain (for it is within
you much more than outside you)
to which life has brought you, are
you not going to find yourself alone
and lost? Men are crowded together
and have to force their way along our
roads, metalled or earthen; even in
the skies they are already beginning
to find themselves cramped. But
in the thousand times vaster and
more complex domain of the mind,
each one of us, the more he is
human (and therefore unique), the
more he is condemned by his very
success to wander, endlessly lost.
You might well have feared, Jean,
that where such a succession of
chances had driven your ship no
other vessel, except by some even

greater chance, would be found.

And it was then, Mademoiselle, in that very habitation of souls in which it seemed impossible that two beings should find one another, that you, like the princess in a fairy story, quite naturally appeared. That, among some thousands of human beings, the eyes of two individuals should meet is in itself a remarkable and precious coincidence: what, then, can we say when it is two minds that meet?

While you, Jean, were engaged in the long circumnavigation during which the real core of every living creature – its power to love – was maturing within you, you, Mademoiselle, were following a different curve, the rhythm of whose approach was nevertheless wonderfully harmonized; and so the two of you were passing through those successive cycles whose culmination we are witnessing here today.

Through your family origins you, too, blossomed on a stem whose roots lie deep in one of France's ancient provinces – Touraine instead of Auvergne – which has about it something warmer and gentler; and, to crown this, you had that finishing touch which only the atmosphere of Paris can give. From your childhood you, too, learnt to revere that same historic academy and the exact science of honourable warfare. In a circle of three children – which included yet another Jacqueline – with an exceptional mother, you, too,

received that generously liberal up-
bringing, firmly based on Christian
principles, which has given so wonderfully harmonious a balance to
your development. And so it was –
with how astonishing a symmetry in
your destinies – that, without realiz-
ing it, you were gradually moving
towards your meeting with the man
who, in equal ignorance, was moving
towards you.

I referred, a moment ago, to fairy
tales. Who was the fairy who, without ever breaking her thread, worked
alone to weave today into one perfect whole the double web of your
two lives?

Was it only chance that blindly
worked this miracle? Must we really
resign ourselves to believing that the

value of the loveliest things around us depends simply on what is unpredictable, unusual, and in consequence impermanent, in the confluence of the elements from which they seem to us to have emerged?

True enough, there are days when the world appears to be one vast chaos. Great, indeed, is the confusion; so great that if we look at ourselves we may very well reel with dizziness at the prospect of our very existence. With such heavy odds against us, is it not most improbable that we should find ourselves whole and entire, and living – as single individuals, let alone as two? We wonder, then, whether true wisdom may not consist in holding on to every chance that comes our way, and immediately drawing all we can from it. It would be madness, surely, to take any further risk with the future and to strive after a life that is even more improbable because even more elevated.

For years now, Jean, my work has been such that every day of my life has necessarily been lived under the shadow of the improbability of life's successes. And once again it is this improbability which I meet today when I look at the happiness of both of you together.

So: since you have asked me to speak today, allow me to tell you what, after a long confrontation with the splendid reality of the world, is my dearest and most profound conviction. I began, like everyone else, by being impressed by the superior importance, among events, that must be accorded to what comes lower down the scale, and to the past. Then, unless I was to cease to understand anything that goes on within me or around me, I was obliged to shift my point of view and accord absolute supremacy to the future and the greater.

No, I believe what gives the universe around us its consistence is not the apparent solidity of the ephemeral materials from which bodies are made. Rather is it the flame of organic development which has been running through the world since the beginning of time, constantly building itself up. With all its weight behind it, the world is being impelled upon a centre which lies ahead of it. Far from being impermanent and accidental, it is souls, and alliances of souls, it is the energies of souls, that alone progress infallibly, and it is they alone that will endure.

What is imponderable in the world is greater than what we can handle.

What radiates from living beings is more valuable than their caresses.

What has not yet come is more precious than what is already born.

That is why what I want to say to you now, Jean – what I want to say to both of you – is this:

'If you want, if both of you want, to answer the summons (or respond to the grace, for that is the better word) which comes to you today from God-animated life, then take

your stand confidently and un-
hesitatingly on tangible matter; take
that as an indispensable bulwark –
but, through and above that matter,
put your faith in the bulwark of the
intangible.'

Put your faith in the spirit that lies
behind you; by that I mean the long
series of unions similar to your own
which throughout the ages have
accumulated, to pass on to you, a
great store of healthy vigour, of
wisdom and of freedom. Today this
treasure is entrusted to your keeping.
Remember that you are responsible
for it to God and the universe.

Put your faith, then, in the spirit
that lies ahead of you. Creation never
comes to a halt. It is through you two
that life seeks to prolong itself. Your

union, therefore, must not be a self-enclosed embrace; let it express itself in that deliberate act, infinitely more unifying than any inactivity, which consists in an effort directed towards one and the same, ever-greater, passionately loved, goal.

And finally, in a phrase that sums up all the rest, put your faith in the spirit which dwells between the two of you. You have each offered yourself to the other as a boundless field of understanding, of enrichment, of mutually increased sensibility. You will meet above all by entering into and constantly sharing one another's thoughts, affections, dreams and prayer. There alone, as you know, in spirit which is arrived at through the flesh, you will find no surfeit, no dis-

appointments, no limits. There alone
the skies are ever open for your love;
there alone lies the great road
ahead.

At this very moment can you not
feel this spirit, to which I am urging
you, concentrating upon you; can
you not feel its mantle spread over
you?

The united love of so many kins-
folk and friends gathered together,
the warmth and purity of wishes
transmitted, through some subtle
medium, from Auvergne, from
Touraine or Poitou, and from the
Côte d'Argent, too; the blessings
sent by those whom we no longer
see; and above all the infinite tender-
ness of Him who sees in you two,
forming one, the welding of one

more precious link in his great work of creative union.

In very truth, grander than the external, material ceremonial which surrounds and honours you, it is the accumulated forces of an invisible loving-kindness which fill this church.

I pray that this spiritual ardour may come down upon your nascent love, and preserve it for eternal life. Amen.

14 June 1928

At the Wedding of M. and Mme de la Goublaye de Ménorval

Mademoiselle, Monsieur,

At this moment, when your two lives are being made one in this chapel, I can think of nothing more appropriate nor more valuable to offer you than a few words in praise of unity.

Unity: an abstract term, maybe, in which philosophers delight; and yet it is primarily a very concrete quality with which we all dream of endowing our works and the world around us. To the apparent fragmentation of material elements, to nature's capricious movements, to the irregularity of colour and sound, to the busy confusion of the masses of mankind, and the undisciplined vacillations of our aspirations and thoughts – what is it that, through all that is best in our activities, we are trying to do, if not constantly to introduce a little more unity? Science, art, politics, ethics, thought, mysticism: these are so many different forms of one and the same impulse towards the creation of some harmony; and in that impulse is expressed, through the medium of our human activities, the destiny and, I would even say, the very essence of the universe. Happiness, power, wealth, wisdom, holiness: these are all synonyms for a victory over the many. At the heart of every being lies creation's dream of a principle which will one day give organic form to its fragmented treasures. God is unity.

What conscious line of action, then, will enable us to pursue and attain this divine unity?

Will it, perhaps, be attained by each one of us setting himself up at the heart of his own little world as an exclusive centre of domination and enjoyment? Does our happiness lie in relating to ourselves, to the greatest possible degree, all that lies outside us? Shall we be happy only if we each become our own little god?

That you two should be here today, bride and bridegroom, shows how completely you have been untouched by this illusion of the self as centre. One of the most pernicious hallucinations that life meets as it awakes to intelligence is the closed concentration of the element on itself; and by this you have not been misled. You have seen that the being in each one of us does not contain its own final pole; it represents a particle which is destined to be incorporated in higher syntheses. Your example shows us not the unity of isolation – but the unity of union.

It is the unity of union that you have chosen; and you have chosen well. But this higher unity which is promised to the elements which seek for one another in a common principle that brings them together – how precisely can that unity reach its perfection in you two? How, being two, will you be more truly one? The question brings me to the very point I want to deal with in these few words; and my answer is: 'By never relaxing your effort to become more yourselves by the giving of yourselves.'

Because union brings fulfilment, it can appear to be a final term, a resting-place. In fact, nothing has a greater share of life's incessantly progressive nature. If the elements are to be able to coalesce, they must spend a long time in first developing in themselves those complementary values which can combine with one another. And when at last the elements meet, they still cannot link up with one another except by advancing continually further along the line of their own fulfilment.

True union, as it brings together, so, and precisely so, it differentiates. It is a continual discovery and a continual conquest.

Perhaps my language is a little ponderous, but it is in those terms that I look for an explanation of your past, and of the promise that the future holds for you.

Your past . . . When we look at you, Mademoiselle, in this festive setting – we, your friends, who have so often seen you deep in the study of rocks or maps, we who have followed you in our thoughts through distant and dangerous expeditions – we might well have a vague feeling that your life has gone off at a tangent, and that you have become a different woman. 'What was the good of conquering

this, in order finally to choose *that*?'
And the right answer to our question
is, 'What is the good of *this* except
as a preparation for *that*?' Never,
Mademoiselle, never – should you,
impossible though it be, ever be so
tempted – regret those long hours in
the laboratory, all the careful work
that went into those lengthy reports,
those strenuous journeys through
the forests of Madagascar. During
these adventures of mind and body,
were you not developing in yourself
the perfect companion for a man
who himself – for this is true of you,
the bridegroom, too, is it not? – be-
longs to the race of those who work
for the earth and explore its secrets?
It took life millions of years to
mould, in the work of creation, the

heart and mind that your mother passed on to you, Mademoiselle. And it still called for all the work and all the hazards of your early youth to perfect in you a being with the capacity to give its self.

And now that same law of which I was speaking, which required that each of you should, alone, make ready for union, is again waiting for you to complete one another, each through the other, in union. What will be the never-ended story of your mutual conquest? This is known to God alone, who is about to bless you. But for my part, I can, on the authority of all human experience, assure you of this: that your happiness will depend on the width of the field you allow to your hopes. An affection that is narrowly closed in on itself stifles body and soul. If you are to ensure the uninterrupted progress that is essential to the fruitfulness of your union, you must extend still further the horizons that have bounded the years of your development.

You will be happy, happy as our prayers and wishes would have you be, only if your two lives come together and extend each other, boldly launching themselves upon the future in a passionate drive towards one greater than yourselves.

15 June 1935

At the Wedding of Christine Dresch and Claude-Marie Haardt

My dear Christine, my dear Claude,
  Life is, indeed, full of strange co-
incidences and, perhaps, strange de-
signs. As Christmas was approaching
in the year 1932, when I was accom-
panying Georges-Marie Haardt on a
journey across the deserts of Central
Asia, who would have guessed that
sixteen years later it would fall to me
to address these words to you, as you
in your turn are about to set out on
another great adventure, that of your
two combined lives? And since the
coincidence probably disguises a
secret design of destiny, may not this
plan contained in material things

(or worked out by Providence) be that I should pass on to you both – and more particularly to you, my dear Claude, in the presence of the mother to whom you owe so much – the admonition, the watchword, that your father, that great inspirer and great traveller, continually offered us by his example, mile after mile over the tracks of Asia, as he urged us to press on and keep our eyes fixed on the peaks that towered ahead of us?

He crossed the Sahara, he crossed Africa and China; and these undertakings, each with its different problems, were all (as is every living reality) built upon a solid material structure. Each was carefully worked out with an eye to a precise end.

And yet, beyond any economic goal, it was always towards some sort of distantly envisaged dream that the fleet of trucks and half-tracks followed him as their leader across the sand. For those who were privileged to take part, these expeditions were always to some extent, and will always remain in their memories, the following of a guiding star . . .

My dear Christine, my dear Claude, now that your turn has come, do you too, imitating your father's grand demeanour in a different sphere, enter into life with your feet firmly on the ground but your eyes fixed on what is greater and finer than you. The temptation which besets love, you know, and makes it barren, is to rest upon what is possessed – it is a shared selfishness. To find one another, and to be truly made one, you must seek no other road but that of a strong passion for a common ideal. Between the two of you (and here the very structure of the world forces upon you a law that cannot be broken) – between the two of you, remember, no un-blemished union can exist except in some higher centre which brings you together.

May that centre soon be the child!

And, come what may, may that centre be the excitement and joy of each discovering and completing the other, ever more fully, in heart and mind!

And, above all, may that centre in one way or another (depending on what is your own particular way) be the God before whom and in whom you are on the point of uniting your two lives for ever: God, the only definitive centre of the universe; not the distant God of common formulas, but God in the form in which he must, and strives to, show himself incommunicably to you if only you surrender unconditionally to the inner force which is at this moment operating to bring you together.

21 December 1948

Date Due